What people are saying about...

## *You(th) Ministry*

*"John Maxwell said it well, "Change is inevitable. Growth is optional."
This book, written by two veteran youth workers, is filled with insight that
will both challenge and inspire you to grow. So take the challenge and allow
Adam and Brandon to guide you on a journey toward health in your life
and leadership. I know you, and the students you are called to serve, will
be changed by the journey."*
**Brandon Shanks | Veteran Student Pastor, The Pentecostals of
Apopka**

*"I have worked with Brandon on several youth events and have been
involved with his youth ministry during his tenure at Christian Life Center,
Stockton CA. Brandon is very effective at growing and maintaining a youth
ministry. I know this book will help and bless you."*
**Cortt Chavis | Pastor Truth Chapel, Loganville Ga**

*"The human side of being a youth worker is unmistakably a long and trying
exercise of patience, diligence and energy. This journey can be taxing and
can leave us spiritually and physically spent if we don't obtain the currency
of golden words on this journey. In a setting full of silver, You(th) Ministry
is the gold you need. It is the right word spoken at the right me. I cannot
recommend it highly enough."*
**David McGovern | 15 year Youth Ministry veteran**

*"Research states that it takes anywhere from 21 to 28 days to form a habit.
Success in Student Ministry is often dependent upon our ability as leaders
to create those healthy spiritual habits. This is more than just a book, it is
a journey towards the personal growth that so often precedes our Student
Ministry's spiritual growth. Be prepared...this book will change you!"*
**Noah Watt | Student Pastor and Author of Backstage Student
Ministry**

"*True change originates in the heart. In their new book You(th) Ministry, Brandon Miraflor and Adam Shaw utilize this truth and lead youth workers in self-surgery. If you let it, this book will mentor you to a higher level of ministry health.*"
**Paul Records | Author of The Picture-Book Guide to Youth Ministry.**

"*You(th) Ministry 29" was written by two guys who have successfully ministered to students and young adults over the past decade. Their experience and gleanings from the trenches have resulted in a book that combines Apostolic principles with practical application and is sure to elevate your leadership quotient.*"
**Shay Mann | General Youth President, United Pentecostal Church International**

"*Writing a book is one of the most challenging mountains to climb. Another mountain to conquer, should God grace you with the calling, is effective ministry to budding disciples. Writing from their own effectiveness in ministry, Miraflor and Shaw map out a clear trail and show you how to achieve greater heights. Youth ministry is one of the most difficult of callings yet one of the most rewarding; You(th) Ministry masterfully marks that path to higher ground.*"
**Russ Cripps | Pastor and Author of Thirtyoneanothers**

"*Brandon and Adam have a compiled a wealth of practical information and tools learned from years of student ministry. You(th) Ministry is a great resource and roadmap for new student leaders, but also forces introspection and evaluation for the most experienced student pastor. The book is a powerful tool for anyone who wants to progress their ministry to students.*"
**Shawn Stickler | Pastor and Ontario District Youth President**

"*One of the most important responsibilities of a leader is to define reality. You must know where you are now before you can ever successfully navigate to your intended destination. In "You(th) Ministry 29", Brandon and Adam have created a self awareness guide, a mirror that will help you see who you are, and they have provided practical, Biblical instruction that will help you become the leader you want to be.*"
**Michael Ensey | General Youth Secretary, United Pentecostal Church International**

# YOU(TH) MINISTRY

**BRANDON A. L. MIRAFLOR &
ADAM M SHAW**

WESTBOW
PRESS
A DIVISION OF THOMAS NELSON

WestBow Press books may be ordered through booksellers or by contacting:

WestBow Press
A Division of Thomas Nelson
1663 Liberty Drive
Bloomington, IN 47403
www.westbowpress.com
1-(866) 928-1240

Because of the dynamic nature of the Internet, any web addresses or links contained in this book may have changed since publication and may no longer be valid. The views expressed in this work are solely those of the author and do not necessarily reflect the views of the publisher, and the publisher hereby disclaims any responsibility for them.

Any people depicted in stock imagery provided by Thinkstock are models, and such images are being used for illustrative purposes only.

Certain stock imagery © Thinkstock.

ISBN: 978-1-4497-6148-6 (hc)
ISBN: 978-1-4497-6147-9 (sc)
ISBN: 978-1-4497-6146-2 (e)

Library of Congress Control Number: 2012913884

Printed in the United States of America

WestBow Press rev. date: 08/31/2012

# Contents

Dedication ..........................................................................vii

Brandon's Acknowledgements ...........................................ix

Adam's Acknowledgements................................................xi

Foreword..........................................................................xiii

Introduction.................................................................... xv

VISION.................................................................................1

NOISE..................................................................................3

FORGIVE .............................................................................5

PRAY ...................................................................................9

MINIMALIST.....................................................................11

ASK ...................................................................................15

FAMILY .............................................................................17

COUNSEL..........................................................................19

WRITE...............................................................................23

LISTEN..............................................................................25

INFLUENCE ......................................................................29

EARLY...............................................................................33

STUDY...............................................................................37

R&R...................................................................................39

MUSIC...............................................................................41

GENEROUS .......................................................................43

CONNECT.........................................................................47

TRIANGLE........................................................................49

TRIANGLE 1 .....................................................................51

TRIANGLE 2 .....................................................................55

TRIANGLE 3 .....................................................................57

GRATEFUL ........................................................................61

DELEGATE ............................................................................65
TRUST....................................................................................69
VALUE ..................................................................................73
VISIT......................................................................................77
PULL THE TRIGGER...........................................................79
LEGACY ...............................................................................83
DREAMS ..............................................................................85
REPEAT ................................................................................89

References ............................................................................91

# Dedication

*We dedicate this book to every youth pastor who, regardless of title or income, works tirelessly in the trenches of youth ministry leading, reaching, teaching, praying with and for thousands of students. You are our heroes. Your work is vitally important to the future of the church and the eternal destinies of every youth you meet.*

# Brandon's Acknowledgements

Thanks to:

Amy. You're the only wife I've got or ever will have. You are my whole existence, and I will love you until my very last breath. What we have is perfect.

Jacob and Evelyn for being the most amazing children a parent could ever ask for. You are my greatest gift, my treasure. Love you with all my heart.

Adam Shaw for being a friend and for the countless hours we spent creating this book. If you hadn't helped with this project I would have completely messed it up and you know that's the truth.

Mom and Dad for your undying love and enduring support.

Ron and Pam Wollmer for your constant support of my family and of me.

David and Bryony Sowers for your love, prayers, and support. Your encouragement was a breath of fresh air.

Scott and Bonnie Mearns for your patience and for doing such a wonderful job with editing.

Eli Lopez for always believing in me and for teaching me how to properly do youth ministry with excellence.

Nathaniel Haney, and the entire Haney family, for backing me up and allowing me to do youth ministry at Christian Life Center.

Robert Johnson for your patience with me and for the amazing cover design.

David McGovern for coming up the brilliant and creative book title.

Monte Young for steering me in the right direction with this project and connecting me with WestBow press. I owe you sir.

All the extraordinarily godly men and women who have invested in me and my ministry throughout the years. There are too many of you to name.

# Adam's Acknowledgements

*Stephanie: Thanks for being an amazing support and friend through this whole project, for reading the manuscript and motivating me when I got tired. You add so much value to my life and ministry. Your hard work and sacrifice has provided me with the opportunity to pursue my dreams. I love you so much.*

*Mom and Dad: Thanks for being incredible, loving and supporting parents who built a Christ-centered home and taught me how to follow Jesus.*

*Brandon Miraflor: Thanks for inviting me to write this project with you. You're a great leader and even better friend.*

*Lifepoint Church and Revolution Youth: You are the best church and youth group on the planet! Together we are going to change the Hamilton region for Jesus.*

*Ontario District: From my close friends to my leaders my collective experience with you has shaped my ministry. Living in community with you has provided me with more than a network of lifelong friends, you're my brothers in arms.*

# Foreword

You hold in your hands a unique little book from a couple of guys who have an obvious passion and a proven track record in Youth Ministry—or as they put it, You(th) Ministry. I like that concept, because youth ministry—or any type of ministry—must become *yours* if it is to impact anyone else. Not yours in the sense of taking the credit, basking in the spotlight, or believing your own press releases, but yours in the sense of *paying the price* to become a leader that God can use for His glory.

Leadership expert John C. Maxwell (and what Forward to a book on leadership would be complete without an obligatory quote from leadership expert John C. Maxwell?) often states that *"leadership is influence."* I agree; we must lead in such a way as to influence those who follow us. And yet, all of the human influence in the world is no match for the deep spiritual problems that plague the generation now living in the early years of the twenty-first century. So what we really need is influence with *God*—and that does not come from mastering a certain set of skills, but from mastering oneself. Real ministry is not just about *what you do*, but about *who you are*.

In Youth Ministry, leaders often concentrate on the competence of their team and the chemistry of their program to get the job done—and these are worthy goals. In fact, you will read some great ideas in this book that will certainly help you in those areas. But the "big idea" here is not about competence or chemistry, but about *character*. By meditating on these twenty-nine principles and accepting each challenge given by the authors, you will grow *yourself* . . . and then effective Youth Ministry is sure to be the result, once effective You(th) Ministry is in place.

Don't let the size of this book fool you. To read it right is going to take you some time, because it isn't about *technique* but about *transformation*. I assure you it will be time well spent.

Thank you, Brandon and Adam, for "getting it" . . . and thank you as well for "sharing it." We will all be better for having taken the journey with you.

Raymond Woodward
Lead Pastor
Capital Community Church
Fredericton, New Brunswick

# Introduction

Welcome to You(th) Ministry! We're so glad that you've joined us on this journey. In fact, don't think of this as a book; it's your roadmap, your field notes to becoming a better youth leader/pastor. Use this book as an advisor. It will guide you on your journey to becoming an effective and truly productive youth worker. This book is designed to focus on the driving force of your ministry: you. True change can only come from the inside. Your youth ministry will only be as healthy and effective as you are. Hence, the title You(th) Ministry.

There's a new workout program that's taking the world by storm. It's called CrossFit. A total body workout program, its main goal is to produce functional fitness. In essence, its specialty is that it doesn't specialize in anything. It hits every area of your body to make you faster, stronger, more explosive. This is the toughest form of training you can do. CrossFit is the antithesis of bodybuilding. Bodybuilding is about aesthetics; CrossFit is about performance. It's not about looking good. It's about being good.

This next example may seem like an odd illustration for youth workers who have been called to bring the peace and wholeness of God to the lives of troubled students. But the truest example of where functional fitness comes into play is the fight game. Really, there is no other sport that is more like ministry than the fight game. You are not trying to score a touchdown or dunk a ball in ministry. You're trying to win a war. You are locked in a cage with culture and your own sinful nature. The dude staring at you from the other side of the octagon is the guy the Scripture describes as the devil. He wants nothing more than to win and destroy God's creation. You're not fighting for a belt but for students. You need to be able to grind it out and to beat him up if you want to win. There is no decision; you are either going to knock him out or you're going to submit to him, or else he's going to do the same to you. Therefore, you cannot afford to look flashy; you've got to actually be a good fighter.

This example is not an endorsement of any one sport or organization, but it's a statement of fact. Youth ministry is a fight. You are in a fight, and our goal is to make you strong so that you can win this fight and gain more students for Christ.

Adam: I remember the first time I tried working out with functional fitness. I had been going to the gym for about three months. I'd lost some weight and was starting to post up what I thought were pretty good numbers in my weight training. As part of my membership, I was eligible to receive a free session with a personal trainer. I was pretty stoked to show the trainer how good I was and how much I knew about working out. If he thought he was going to break me, he was wrong. Well, let's just say I was the one who was wrong—really, really wrong, some may even say delusional. As this behemoth of a human being tortured me through a battery of squats, sprints, cleans, pushups, and burpees, I became painfully aware that heavy squats didn't amount to, well, squat. Bad puns aside, halfway through the workout, my face turned an interesting shade of green. Long story short, I turn to "trainer from former Soviet bloc country" and declared that I needed to use the bathroom. He finally relented, and I sprinted toward the locker room. No sooner did I burst through the stall door when what I ate that day began to be wildly ejected from my body. It was bad. See, my problem was I was really good at a couple of things, but when it came time to put them together and use my fitness in a functional, real-world way, I failed.

Most everyone is given a set of skills, talents, and abilities; however, they are not always the keys to having success in youth ministry. There are a lot of practical habits that even the most skilled and talented youth workers must obtain to maximize their potential and be effective leaders.

So, You(th) Ministry is designed to be read one "challenge" at a time. Read each Bible study, and then begin the process of executing the challenge posed at the end. That's it. Sounds simple, but if you will make your way through this entire book, you will not be the same youth leader you are right now.

This book is short, but that doesn't mean it's easy. We are going to hit every area of your life: your relationships, your creativity, your management. We want you to partner with us and go on a journey to transform yourself and your student ministry.

—

Brandon and Adam

# VISION

**Read:** Matthew 28

**Focus Text:** Matthew 28:18-20 (NLT)
"Jesus came and told his disciples, 'I have been given all authority in heaven and on earth. Therefore, go and make disciples of all the nations, baptizing them in the name of the Father and the Son and the Holy Spirit. Teach these new disciples to obey all the commands I have given you. And be sure of this: I am with you always, even to the end of the age.'"

There are multiple metaphors to spiritual life and multiple examples of spiritual leaders in scripture. Yet regardless of the type, shadow, or circumstance, there is a commonality in each successful picture of leadership: vision. If you are leading people you need to not only be taking them somewhere, but you also must have a plan to get them to that destination. All of us know the power and importance of a well-crafted vision statement and a properly developed ministry plan. Thus, the purpose of this chapter is not to get you to develop a vision but to refine the one you already have so that it makes your ministry more effective.

Here are some vision refinement tips:

You need to make sure the vision fits the cultural context where God has placed you. All of us follow great church movements and ministries that are doing amazing things. Those amazing things are being done because, through the power of the Holy Spirit, those churches have tapped into the culture of their community and are presenting the

Gospel in their unique context. They literally have become missionaries to their communities. While they may have ideas that are very creative, their ability to weave themselves into the fabric of their community is the key to success.

You need to develop a vision that is in line with the language, culture, and mission of your church. While it may seem easy to borrow the language, culture, and mission statement of "Church X", that's not cool and it's never a good idea. God has not called you to recreate "brand x" in your student ministry, he's called you to contextualize the mission and vision of the greater local church into your youth ministry. So when students graduate out of your youth ministry they're not walking into a different church. Your vision will only be effective if it falls in line with the language and culture of the local church that God has called you to lead in.

We are not called to create another church. We are called to create a youth ministry arm that supports what the senior pastor is doing. You can never supersede the vision of your pastor! If you refuse to adopt this principle, you will become frustrated and eventually burnout. There's a myth out there in youth ministry which says that if I line up with my pastor's vision, then everything I do is going to look old and frumpy, I'm not going to be able to do new worship songs, utilize creative elements in my youth room, etc. But, the truth is, you can be a success with what God has put in your pastor's hand.

Too often youth workers have no clue as to the overarching vision of their local church. If you find yourself in this position, all you have to do is ask.

**The Challenge:**
Contact your senior pastor or the leader you report to directly, and communicate that you're going over the mission and purpose of the youth ministry and that you want to meet with him/her about what he/she would like to see happen the next 6-12 months.

The vision of our Pastor

# NOISE

**Read:** Luke 5:1-16

**Focus Text:** Luke 5:16 (NIV)
"But Jesus often withdrew to lonely places and prayed."

Noise. "Noise" comes from the Latin word "nausea"[1], which metaphorically means "disgust, annoyance, discomfort." Literally, it means "seasickness."[2] That's interesting because its been reported that noise pollution can cause annoyance and aggression, high blood pressure, high stress levels, tinnitus, and hearing loss. It can also cause sleep disturbances, forgetfulness, severe depression, and at times, panic attacks![3] Because of the potentially devastating effects of noise, there are whole organizations dedicated to lowering the amount of noise in public spaces. Your life is probably pretty noisy. The constant pinging of your phone and an avalanche of all things digital can disrupt your spiritual and emotional equilibriums and make you feel, well, sick. Have you ever thought that maybe you should turn the volume down?

Adam: "Sometimes my mind feels numb from all the noise in my life. It seems like by the end of my day the deluge of emails, calls, texts, tweets, and status updates leaves me shell-shocked. Like a hyperactive squirrel, I run from one thing to the next, bouncing from proverbial

---

[1]  Denis Howe. noise.Dictionary.com; *The Free On-line Dictionary of Computing*. http://dictionary.reference.com/browse/noise.

[2]  Denis Howe. nausea.Dictionary.com; *The Free On-line Dictionary of Computing*. http://dictionary.reference.com/browse/nausea.

[3]  "Noise pollution" *Wikipedia, the free encyclopedia.* http://en.wikipedia.org/wiki/Noise_pollution#cite_note-0.

tree to proverbial tree. It leaves me feeling busy, but the reality is that sometimes I don't accomplish very much.

"When I get quiet, I hear God, and I realize my emptiness. Jesus confronts me with my life and what I've built with it. Here is where I find which things in my life are precious stones and which are wood, hay, and stubble. When I am silent, and when I silence the deluge of voices in my world, I hear his voice and it brings me what I crave: clarity and revelation—those moments where God, in his might, splendor, holiness, and love intersects with my cloudy heart and numb mind. All of a sudden I see him. In those moments I am restored; my vision renewed and my heart strengthened."

In the wild and crazy world of youth ministry, time with God and time away from noise are more valuable than gold or a new iPad (which is pretty much the same thing). Silence will reveal the spiritual emptiness in you that you've been filling with noise. Awareness of your own emptiness will produce a restlessness and hunger for more from God, but these moments will never come if you don't make them happen. You must regularly practice the discipline of spending time with God and silencing other voices.

This is the example of Jesus. In our text, we read that after performing the miracle, Jesus abandoned the crowd and went into the wilderness to pray. What's in the wilderness? Nothing. That was exactly the point. See, as God, he could do all things, but as a man he needed to break away from the noise and pray so that he would be renewed.

**The Challenge:**
Take a break from all things digital. Take your Bible, a pen, and a notebook and spend at least two hours reading, writing, and reflecting on God's Word in total silence.

# FORGIVE

**Read:** Matthew 18:21-35

**Focus Text:** Matthew 18:33 (NLT)
"Shouldn't you have mercy on your fellow servant, just as I had mercy on you?"

Adam: "I was thirteen. I stood outside my dad's office door. Despite the fact that the door was closed and thick walls stood between the office and the hallway, I still heard the shouts. The shouts and the thuds as the man slammed his fist on to my dad's desk again and again and again, violently punctuating his tirade against my father. He railed against my father's leadership, his vision, his theology, and even his character. The accusations were totally unfounded. The man had simply decided he no longer liked some of our beliefs and thought that since he was a leader and had given some money to the ministry, he could bully my father into "seeing it his way." My dad was driven by principle, not money, so he refused to compromise, which resulted in the man losing his temper after our Sunday evening service. The man was our music director. When you're a church planter, your music guy is vital. We had no one who could take his place. This hurt us. It wasn't fair. We'd worked so hard, and it seemed like we had finally been getting some momentum. Now we were about to suffer a setback. Stuff like this wasn't supposed to happen. We were supposed to have revival. No one in the church should act like that. I remember after hearing all I could stand, I went back into the auditorium and lay facedown on the carpet, in the back row of the church, and sobbed. I sobbed and prayed that God would turn this situation around, that this man would repent and we could go back to normal. It didn't happen. My sadness turned to anger. Anger turned to bitterness tinged with hatred. Those feelings stuck with me. Trauma had made me emotionally and spiritually sick."

In order to build a healthy team and youth ministry, you must be healthy. If you serve out of your dysfunction, then there will be parts of your ministry that will be dysfunctional. Notice we didn't say pain. While overcoming pain is best, pain is okay because it humanizes you and helps you empathize with the brokenness in your students. But dysfunction breaks you. Bitter people are often suspicious of others' motives and intentions. You will struggle with trusting your staff, your pastor, and your students' parents all because you refuse to FORGIVE that one person! What's worse, your dysfunction can cause you to break others. Anger and bitterness always spread; they are never satisfied to stay in one location.

Adam: "Over five years had passed. I had long since moved from that small church. My dad was now the pastor at a larger church, and for the first time, he was actually getting paid to preach. I had moved to New Brunswick so that I could attend Bible College. I went to classes Monday through Friday and spoke at churches in New Brunswick, Nova Scotia, or Maine on weekends. People liked me. I had a wonderful girlfriend (who later became my wife), and I was the president of my first year class. Yet despite all of these new and fresh changes, a root of bitterness was lurking deep within my heart. Its branches still had a stranglehold on my attitude and my trust. Then something happened; I remember it like it was yesterday. I sat in the passenger seat of my girlfriend's 1994 Saturn LS1, and with rapt attention, listened to a preaching cd from a conference. The pastor speaking was telling his story of bitterness and how he'd had to forgive. Conviction burned in my conscience as God confronted me with the hatred I had been justifying. As I began to pray and cry out to God to heal the infected wound of my heart, the power of the Holy Spirit exploded in that car. I became a wreck. I slumped over in my seat sobbing. As I prayed, God reached into my heart and ripped out that root of bitterness. I distinctly remember that supernatural moment because I instantly began to pray that God would forgive and save the man who had hurt me. I would love to say that after that moment I never had another trust issue and my attitude was always right, but that would not be reality. There were times when memories would flood back. Each time they did, I would remind myself of that earth-shattering moment I had with God, and would make a choice to forgive. Forgiveness is a choice. I choose to not have you owe me anymore."

When we refuse to forgive, we build an altar to our pain and worship it every day.

**The Challenge:**
Find someone you have harbored negative feelings toward, and take the first step in releasing them.

# PRAY

**Read:** John 17:6-19

**Focus Text:** John 17:9-10 (NLT)
"My prayer is not for the world, but for those you have given me, because they belong to you. All who are mine belong to you, and you have given them to me, so they bring me glory."

Take some time today and pray for the youth in your youth ministry. As you will see in "Listen," the key to knowing the needs within your youth ministry is immersion. You've got to be a student of their culture and find out what their needs are. Don't simply pray for generic, overall well-being, but get specific. Visualize their faces as they're going through their day. You will be amazed as you begin to pray how a whole other burden will begin to come on you.

Our Focus Text provides an intimate picture into Christ's love for his disciples. His prayer was that the Father would intervene in some very specific ways. Read again through the prayer of Jesus in John 17. Use that prayer as your model to pray for your young people.

**The Challenge:**
Create a list with names of the students you pastor, and pray for them everyday. Remember to also pray for those who serve with you in leadership.

# MINIMALIST

**Read:** Hebrews 12:1-2

**Focus Text:** Hebrews 12:1 (ESV)
"Therefore, since we are surrounded by so great a cloud of witnesses, let us also lay aside every weight, and sin which clings so closely, and let us run with endurance the race that is set before us."

Brandon: "As I travel, the first question I usually get asked when being picked up at the airport is, 'Is that all you have?!' And with much satisfaction, I smile and say, 'Yes.' I refuse to check my bags at the airport. I am a die-hard minimalist. I can go for two to three weeks on a twenty-inch carry-on bag. I intentionally buy accessories and employ packing methods that allow me to live out this minimalist ideal.

"When it comes to traveling and being a minimalist, there are several keys. First, always travel with a small bag. The bag matters because the bigger the bag the more you will have the urge to fill it. Baggage makes you slow. Second, have a plan. I use a checklist that I've refined throughout the years. This ensures that I will not pack anything I do not need, and I won't forget something I do need. And, third, be conservative. Minimize the amount of toiletries you bring, and when it comes to packing clothing, don't get fancy and flashy; bring clothes that are neutral and interchangeable. Find pieces that you can use multiple times. These simple keys allow me to 'GO' at anytime."

Are you a ministry minimalist? You should be.

We're not saying you need to change your packing style. However, we all could probably lean up our ministry models and systems. The scripture seems to indicate that there are things that are sin and things that just slow you down. In ministry, as with your personal life, there are things that might not be wrong but they're slowing down your effectiveness. There's a good chance your youth ministry has too many "bags" and you need to throw some things aside.

Here are some questions you should consider. Ministry leadership expert Andy Stanley asks, "Where are you manufacturing energy?" In other words, what things are you constantly having to resurrect? What things are dead that you're constantly trying to breathe new life into? What things have your youth ministry always done that you secretly despise? STOP DOING THOSE THINGS!

If you don't stop, you're wasting your time. If you hate it, everybody else hates it, and it's not effective. If you do it just because you've always done it, but you're constantly trying to create energy and excitement around it, then you've got to stop doing it. Seriously, just stop!

That was the easy part.

Once you've eliminated the dead weight, you've got a more difficult task ahead of you. What are you going to do with what is good, but not great? In other words, what things are you investing time and resources in that, while they are good, are just taking away time and resources from the things that are your definitive winners?

We are all really good at identifying things in our ministries that are really bad, but we go to the next level in our ministries when we decide to stop doing the things that are just okay and only do the things that are amazing.

Part of this is also doing only what fits the size and resources of your ministry. While we can all learn from churches and ministries larger than ours, and while we must always plan for the future, we must also be realistic about what we are able to do right now. By extending your ministry in too many directions, you run the risk of failing to execute anything well. You can also stretch your resources so thin that you don't have the necessary cash to execute your vision. Add a program only when you are able fully launch it. Then, launch it and run it "lean."

The challenge below may sound easy, but some parts of it will be truly challenging. Some of the programs that need to be cut may be your pet projects which are no longer as effective as they used to be. The key is to disconnect your emotions and dispassionately review. Remember, the goal is for more young people to meet Jesus and become disciples. Anything that keeps you from that goal is worth refining or cutting.

**The Challenge:**
Balance your life. List the top ten things in your life that you regard as important.

Balance your ministry. List and review all of your programs, processes, and budget items. Meet with your team to get their feedback. What's bad? What's great? What can be improved?

# ASK

**Read:** John 6:1-12

**Focus Text:** John 6:5-6 (ESV)
"Lifting up his eyes, then, and seeing that a large crowd was coming toward him, Jesus said to Philip, 'Where are we to buy bread, so that these people may eat?' He said this to test him, for he himself knew what he would do."

Jesus seldom provided an immediate answer for his disciples. He allowed them to operate within their level of faith, knowledge, and understanding. John, in our Focus Text, stated that Jesus " . . . knew what he would do," but he wanted to see what the disciples would do. By getting them to contribute, Jesus invited them to participate with him in the execution of his miracle. Through this invitation to dialogue, Jesus got his disciples to buy into the solution.

In the Read portion of the scripture, after Jesus asked the disciples what to do, the next thing he said was, "Make them sit down." Is that it? No! Rather, Jesus gave them an ownership stake in the miracle by allowing them to be a part of its execution.

Sometimes in leadership, you ask a question already knowing the answer. In your heart, you may know what you would do, but like Jesus, you invite your team to have a dialogue about the problem and its possible solution. By allowing your team to identify the problem, discuss a solution, and participate in the execution, you maximize buy-in and loyalty to the vision. But before you get to the execution stage, you need to ask some questions.

15

Think of an issue that is challenging you right now in your youth ministry. What is the result you want to see in this situation? Now think of questions you can ask your team about the situation that will bring about a positive solution. By doing this, you allow them to take ownership of and have a part in the "miracle."

**The Challenge:**
In your next team meeting, lead the team to the right decision by asking a series of questions that will lead them to both define the issue and come up with a solution. Avoid the urge to constantly add your input to the discussion; let the conversation play out.

# FAMILY

**Read:** 1 Timothy 3:1-13

**Focus Text:** 1 Timothy 3:4-5 (NLT)
"He must manage his own family well, having children who respect and obey him. For if a man cannot manage his own household, how can he take care of God's church?"

Family has been, and always will be, the foundation of pastoral ministry. The only way you can live up to the Apostle Paul's family requirements for ministry is by taking the time to nurture and love your family. There is no one else who can, or will, do this for you. It's something that takes time and focus, but it will ultimately bring about the health that will allow you to adequately lead your youth ministry.

Brandon: "I remember back in the summer of 1999, when I first started working in youth ministry. I was eighteen, single, and without a care in the world. I could come and go as I pleased. I could hang with the youth because I was a youth. But when I got married at age twenty-four, everything began to change. In addition to being a youth worker, I was a husband. A couple of years later, my wife and I had our first child, our energetic son Jacob, and the challenge of juggling family and ministry became even greater. A few years ago, my beautiful, amazing daughter Evelyn popped into my world and stole my heart. Now, as a husband and father, the responsibility of taking care of my family is ultimately more important than my ministry. They have become my ministry. No, I'll never stop being a youth worker, but my first priority is my family."

Whether you're married with kids or single, family matters. There may come a day when you will no longer be a youth worker, and all that "stuff" that was so important and had to get done will be gone. But your family will still be there.

**The Challenge:**
Contact your family members today and tell them how much you love, appreciate, and value them.

# COUNSEL

**Read:** Proverbs 11:13-16

**Focus Text:** Proverbs 11:14 (NKJV)
"Where there is no counsel, the people fall;
But in the multitude of counselors there is safety."

He stepped to the podium, and his voice shook as he admitted that the allegations were true. The moral failure was not just a bad rumor. The hushed whispers of apparent gossip swirling around the organization were not just bored, idle, water-cooler talk. It was the cold, hard truth. He had failed. No matter his calling; no matter how chosen or talented he was, it was all over.

There is a deep need for honest, truthful ministers who actually have integrity, but increasingly, pastors are falling prey to scandal. We have all reeled in shock and horror as our ministry-hero fell. You know the guy; his speaking skills and creative talents made you just a little jealous. His moment of indiscretion and temptation completely ruined a lifetime of work, sacrifice, and effort. We've all seen it.

No matter who it happens to, it always starts the same way: with isolation. Isolation always equals bad decisions. They got so big, so proud, that they decided they could do it alone. Surrounded by yes-men, or lacking wise counselors and accountability, their character remained unchecked and issues remained unresolved.

The scripture is clear: you've got to have ethics if you want to be a good leader.

Titus 1:7-8 (ESV)

"For an overseer, as God's steward, must be above reproach. He must not be arrogant or quick-tempered or a drunkard or violent or greedy for gain, but hospitable, a lover of good, self-controlled, upright, holy, and disciplined."

Depth of character is key in determining your success as a leader. Take a few minutes right now and examine your character. Are there any cracks? Where are the flaws?

So many times throughout your journey in ministry, you will find yourself in the position where you need counsel. The decisions that present themselves to us are often tedious and not always black and white. From the Focus Text, we understand that there is safety and wisdom in a multitude of counselors.

Counsel is good, not just because it brings you good advice and great ideas, but it also brings to the surface your vulnerabilities. Counsel forces you to admit that you don't have all the answers; it is a foundation that invites another to keep you accountable.

A counselor is really someone who keeps you in check, challenges your presuppositions, and makes sure you follow through. A good, godly counselor loves you so much they'll call you on your junk and let you know when you're being stupid.

Build systems into your life which will help people keep you accountable. If you can't, why not? What are you afraid of? Is it the loss of control, or is it what they will find?

There are three types of counselors you need in your life: rabbis, peers, and disciples.

A "rabbi" is a wise elder, someone who has been where you are, who's made some mistakes, but has learned how to be a success. The rabbi plays the role of teacher and mentor. He/she instructs you with practical principles and provides fatherly/motherly accountability. The key to a functioning rabbi relationship is submission. He or she is going to call you on your junk, and sometimes you're going to despise the experience. In those times, you must be humble enough to receive correction and a rebuke. Understand that your rabbi is looking out for your best interest. The coward's way out is to simply find a new rabbi when the current one doesn't tell him what he wants to hear. A true leader is willing to follow as much as he leads.

Your peers are your "bro's," your buddies, the guys/girls in the trenches with you. Your contemporaries provide valuable insight because they see things from a different perspective. This is why it's so important to have a diverse peer group. Do not seek to be friends only with people just like you, but build relationships from diverse cultural and ideological backgrounds.

Disciples are those you lead. Seek advice from your followers; they provide neat insight since they are usually not your equals in experience and authority. They can provide feedback on the effectiveness of your ideas and your leadership. It's okay if those who follow you see that you don't have all the answers. By asking questions, you show that a leader doesn't have to know everything; he or she just needs to be able to ask the right questions.

**The Challenge:**
Take a moment to pray, then make a list of righteous voices you need speaking into your life in order to reach the dreams and goals God has placed in you.

Rabbis (elders):

_____

_____

_____

Peers (your contemporaries):

_____

_____

_____

Disciples (those you are mentoring):

_____

_____

_____

# WRITE

**Read:** 1 Kings 19:9-18

**Focus Text:** 1 Kings 19:12 (NKJV)
"And after the earthquake a fire, but the Lord was not in the fire; and after the fire a still small voice."

Adam: "Ever since I was a little kid, Beverly Dummitt has not missed my birthday. She is the wife of a pastor at a neighboring church. That church, and especially the Dummitt family, was incredibly kind to me. Growing up in a church planter's home, my own church was quite small, so connecting to a strong and stable church and youth ministry was important to my spiritual health. One of the ways I was made to feel connected was through the cards I would receive from Sis. Dummitt on my birthdays. They were always full of stickers with little positive messages and a handwritten note where she would tell me how proud she was of me and how much God was going to use me. Even when my family moved and my dad became pastor of a larger church, Sis. Dummitt kept sending birthday cards. When I moved to the other side of the country to go to college, and even after I got married, the cards continued. Though I'm a grown man (with the back hair to prove it), there's something about a card, full of stickers that say "Way to go!" or "You're the best," that makes me feel pretty awesome. Maybe it was the time she devoted to sending the cards. She had to go to a store, buy the card, take the time to write in it, seal the envelope, and put in the mail. Maybe it was the fact that her care for me was expressed with something tangible."

The Read section of this chapter gives us a snapshot of one of the prophet Elijah's lowest moments. At this time, Elijah's life is chaotic, noisy, and very frightening. So, he runs to a cave and hides, and it is there he has an encounter with God. The amazing thing about Elijah's encounter is that God chooses to speak, not in the same chaotic way that every other voice in Elijah's life is speaking, but in a still, small voice. That quiet voice broke through the craziness of his life and gave him clarity.

Somewhere along the line, culture has lost the art of making things personal. We live in such a digitally-saturated world, and we are so used to electronic communication that it can take a lot just to get students' attention. The constant swarm of digital messages they encounter every day can, at times, cause our voices to get lost. Ours are just lone voices in the cacophony of life noise. Our challenge is finding a way to break through. Handwritten communication may be old school, but it is one way to make your "voice" be heard.

**The Challenge:**
Write one note or card to one guy and one girl in your youth ministry today. We're talking snail mail; a simple postcard in the mailbox will do the trick. Make it short like a text. Think 140 characters. Who will you write to today?

_____

_____

# LISTEN

**Read:** Mark 10:46-52

**Focus Text:** Mark 10:51 (ESV)
"And Jesus said to him, 'What do you want me to do for you?' And the blind man said to him, 'Rabbi, let me recover my sight.'"

In December 2011, Coca Cola did the unthinkable: they changed the color of their cans! (Gasp!) Loyal Coke fans went absolutely ballistic. They claimed everything from "it confused them", to "it tasted different" to "it's just a sacrilege."[4] Now, before you roll your eyes at finicky consumers, take a moment and consider the following: Coca Cola has been around since 1886, and for decades it has done a masterful job at making its product more than a beverage. Coke has tied its brand to thousands of meaningful life experiences, such as family picnics, days at the beach, or Christmas get-togethers. For lifelong consumers, the Coke brand represents personal life experiences, and the sugary carbonated beverage is intertwined with wonderful memories. So, imagine the Coke fans' dismay when the object that was a partner and facilitator in their holiday cheer suddenly looked radically different. The moment Coke made a unilateral decision without consulting consumers, it broke a cardinal leadership rule; listen to your customer.

Blind Bartimaeus was not part of the inner circle; he was not giving softball answers. He was not jostling for political position either. He

---

[4]   Mike Esterl. "A Frosty Reception For Coca-Cola's White Christmas Cans". http://online.wsj.com/article/SB10001424052970204012004577070521211375302.html. (accessed May 30, 2012)

25

just came in his point of need. He fit the description of the type of person Jesus came to reach. There are students right in the middle of the demographic you are trying to reach. Not in the band, not in leadership, they have no political power in your organization yet they still need to be heard.

We have to hear what people are saying, and the best way to do that is to actively listen. The word that comes to my mind is "immersion." Immerse means to fully submerge or to involve deeply. By listening, we don't just mean listening to auditory sounds, we mean getting deep into their world and understanding what it is like.

Adam: "A few years ago, I read a marketing study done by MTV in which they defined the word 'immerse.' The MTV marketing team submerged themselves in a field of research completed in three markets using a small-group discussion format in a 'non-traditional' setting. Using MTV age segments of 12-17 and 18-24, they also performed a quantitative survey with 1,200 respondents. They asked the participants deep life questions. They asked about their most intimate feelings and perspectives. The youth in the survey were asked about their relationships with their parents, their beliefs on religion and philosophy, and their engagement with technology. They were even asked questions about their body image. The result was that MTV got a snapshot of the heart of a 21st century young person. The crazy thing is, at least from our perspective, MTV's intent was 'carnal.' They conducted the research partly to help their advertisers better sell products and partly to help MTV better create programming to suck in teens and young adults. In response to the MTV study, I decided to do some research of my own. I didn't have millions of dollars to sample teens from every socioeconomic background in my city, but I was able to get in a room, ask some questions and just listen. In the process, I had some of the most meaningful conversations I've ever had. The students I talked with said things such as: 'People say judging is bad, but how do I know when judging is wrong? When is it wrong to judge?' They also commented, 'Bullying is a big issue at school, but the focus seems to be solely on homosexuality during anti-bullying week.

So, what's the Christian response? What do I do when I'm faced with pressure for standing up against homosexuality?' They even wanted to know, 'How do I stand up for the Bible, and, at the same time, love everybody like Jesus does?'"

Oftentimes, we think we know what people want and how to deliver it to them, but we may actually be shooting over their heads and not connecting at all. That might be the reason they are not responding to your message. It might not be because "something is wrong with this generation!" It could be that you're not connecting. Take time to get feedback from your youth about how you are doing as a leader, what they want to hear you address next, and what questions they may have. If you think you're so smart and so good that you don't need input from your youth, then you may need to repent of arrogance.

**The Challenge:**
Listen to your students. Meet with a group of students who are not on your team—those who aren't in the band or in leadership—but let them do the talking while you just listen. Ask open-ended questions about their dreams, their fears, and their spirituality. Figure out what their world is like.

# INFLUENCE

**Read:** John 1:35-55

**Focus Text:** John 1:37 (NKJV)
"The two disciples heard him speak, and they followed Jesus."

Attack the desire to be needed. We love being needed. We love being people's only last hope. If you're looking around and saying, "There's no one who can help me. I've got to do this all by myself," stop! Take a look in the mirror, and ask yourself, "Did God really call me to do this all by myself, or is there someone in this ministry who is, or can become, an influencer and a leader?"

Sometimes we don't develop leaders because we like being busy. There's a certain adrenaline rush we get trying to juggle multiple relationships and responsibilities. However, busy is not always better.

Leaders like to be in control. That's why they're leaders. Sometimes though, our greatest strength can also be our greatest weakness. Our desire to control everything can cause us to quickly hit burn-out. You have students in your ministry right now who want to help, who are called to help. They are unformed, undeveloped, raw talent filled with leadership potential. They just need someone to discover them, train them, and empower them. If you can take it one step at a time and influence the influencers, it can pay long term dividends. You weren't called to build an organization; you were called to build people.

Think of it this way. You may have a staff of very qualified adults helping lead your youth ministry, but it's possible you also have some talented students available. While you may need to reevaluate your standard of excellence in order for more students to become involved, in the long run you'll benefit by turning your teen church culture from consumption to production.

When Jesus picked the apostles, they weren't slick at all. They were undereducated and unprepared, but they had a great teacher. After spending three and half years with Jesus, they were ready to change the world. Jesus knew the greatest impact would be made, not by building a fantastic organization, but by developing people who would be able to go and change the world.

As you've read this chapter, the names or faces of a few students have flashed in your mind. You are thinking of the ones everyone wants to be around, the natural leaders who people often look up to. The influencers you're thinking of may not be your first choice as spiritual leaders. Some of them are very positive students who are leaders at school, but they aren't necessarily spiritual leaders or fully involved in the local youth group, but they are there nonetheless. We often feel intimidated because there's a chance we can't "control them."

However, whether they seem interested or not, we can still influence them. Influence is not control; it is simply having an effect on their character or development as they grow in Christ. As a youth worker, you leverage your God-given spiritual authority in their lives, enabling you to tap into their tribes and establish some influence where you would otherwise have no influence. As a youth worker you cannot create peer pressure. Only a peer can create peer pressure, and peer pressure equals influence.

There are usually three different groups within the local youth group; the "fringe," the "there," and the "core." Within each of these levels there are always influencers and peer-to-peer leaders.

We want to challenge you to not be afraid to reach for the influencers in all three groups even if they don't fit the grid or the mold of the preconceived idea of what a youth leader should look like.

**The Challenge:**
Identify one or two influencers and connect with them.

1. _____

2. _____

# EARLY

**Read:** Matthew 25:1-13

**Focus Text:** Matthew 25:11-12 (NIV)
"Later the others also came. 'Lord, Lord,' they said, 'open the door for us!' But he replied, 'Truly I tell you, I don't know you.'"

The five foolish virgins did not take the time to prepare. They procrastinated and were late to the party. As a result, they got left out. The obvious intent of this passage is to admonish us to be plugged into Christ and be ready for eternal life. However, despite the obvious context, there is something to be said about the example of time Jesus used in this parable; specifically, the negative association of being late.

The fact of the matter is, being late is never good. Not showing up on time is a sign of poor leadership. Time is valuable, and time is important. (This is where Adam was tempted to insert a very long philosophical perspective on the nature of time, but Brandon realized that the eyes of 90 percent of everyone reading this book would glaze over. Instead, we simply decided to say: "Time is super important.")

When you break it down, you actually have a very small amount of time in which to do productive things with your day. But here's the deal: not only is your time important; everyone's time is important. Everybody faces limitations on time. Everyone is busy. Everyone is stressed. Everyone has too much on his or her plate. Sorry, you're not that special. Therefore, since everyone is in the same boat, treat everyone's time with respect.

Time is not just something you keep on your watch or hang on the wall, but it is what provides order and space to the universe. And time is limited! You need to use it wisely because it is a resource that can be lost.

Here's the clincher: everybody has the same time resource problems that you do. Since everybody is stretched, and nobody has an unlimited amount of time, the way you treat other people's time affects the way they view you as a leader. If you misuse their time, you may cause them to lose faith in your leadership and maybe even your integrity.

Brandon: "Chronically late people frustrate me to no end because the message they are sending me is, 'Your time is not important to me; it is not as valuable as mine. What is going on in my life and my world is more important than what's happening in yours, so I get to walk into our appointment whenever I want.' When you show up late, you send a negative message to those you lead and to those you follow. This is why, as a leader, you need to be time conscious.

"If you have a 7 o'clock appointment, and you arrive at 7:01, then you are late. At 6:59 you are early. You have only 60 seconds to be on time. If you will start looking at time this way, you will begin to respect and value others' time more.

"You need to get this ingrained in your head. As a leader, if your meeting starts at 7:00, don't walk in the door at 7:00. You need to be there early, because it will take time to do things, such as, unlock and open the doors and get settled and ready to run a meeting. If you walk in at 7:00, when the meeting is supposed to begin, you will waste others' precious time.

"I know, I know. At some point we've all been late for an appointment. It happens. But what bugs me and drives me nuts is we live in a culture that rewards people who are late. Here's what I mean. If Adam is early to every meeting by five to 10 minutes, we consider him punctual and reliable, and the meeting can start on time. However, if we also have

Brandon, who shows up five to 10 minutes late, he is rewarded by us delaying the start of the meeting until he arrives. We do this because we really want Brandon to be there. We want him to be informed and involved in what's going on. We also want him to feel connected; plus, we don't want to have to recap for him the 10 minutes of the meeting he missed. By accommodating Brandon's tardiness, we actually enable his inefficiencies and deficiencies, and we help to perpetuate his inability to be organized and on time."

Here's an alternative to the scenario. When the meeting is scheduled, everyone plans to get there 10 minutes early, so that we actually start the meeting on time. At one minute past the scheduled meeting start time, we are already taking care of business. All of the sudden, you have a culture shift. Brandon walks into the meeting 10 minutes late. Guess what? He's out of the loop; he may even have to get some notes from another staff member. Brandon's like, "Oh, snap! Next week I had better be there early."

Many times when we are late, we use the excuse, "I've been busy." This is not completely honest. The truth is, we did not make it a priority; the people we were dealing with were not important enough to us. If somebody approached you on a very busy day and told you to call him or her at 1 o'clock to be told the location of $1,000,000, would you call? Of course you would! Why? Because you would make it a priority.

Yes, you are busy, but you can still plan ahead and be organized enough to be there 10 minutes early. You should do it not only because it's the right thing to do, but also because you want others to know that you value them and their time, and that they are a priority to you and God.

As you become known for punctuality, it will change the way people view you as a leader. It will also change the way you view yourself. Studies show that people who are punctual are considered reliable and more trustworthy.

We understand the church was never meant to be a "business." We were never meant to sell widgets or produce clones. However, we do recognize that there is a business and professional side to ministry. We want to always present ourselves in a professional manner that not only shows we are organized and know what we're doing, but also says, "You are important to us."

When visitors and guests come in contact with you, they're going to come in contact with excellence. As is often the case, their lives may be in disarray. We want them to come in contact with something that is different and stands out. When you tell your youth that you're going to meet them for Bible study at 3 o'clock, you should be there at least 10 minutes early. That way they realize you are someone they can actually trust, lean on, and look to because you keep your word. Being "on time" is a big part of being a leader.

**The Challenge:**
Show up 10 minutes early for every appointment today.

# STUDY

**Read:** Mark 8:27-33

**Focus Text:** Mark 8:31 (NIV)
"He then began to teach them...."

Brandon: "As a kid growing up, I went to Sunday School every Sunday. I also had the privilege of going to a private Christian school. I came from a two-parent home where the Bible was often open. It is safe to say that I was Biblically educated."

However, today youth pastors are dealing with youth that have very little Biblical knowledge, and in some cases, they have none. We are not here to bemoan that things have changed. It's how things are now, but we don't have to leave things the way they are. By increasing your students' Biblical knowledge, you help them progress to the next level in their walk with Jesus Christ.

A great place to start is by immersing students in the narrative of scripture. The Bible is not just a book of philosophical and theological arguments; it's a book of stories about real people who did their best to follow God. There are heroes, villains, saints, and sinners—sometimes, all wrapped up in a single character. God, in his sovereign wisdom, works out his master story through the flawed characters of the Bible, who earnestly sought God. In the narrative of scripture, we find pictures and symbols of Jesus and we also discover ourselves.

When students discover both Christ and themselves in the pages of Scripture, it is a life-changing revelation. Increasing biblical literacy is a cornerstone of discipleship. The more a student knows the Word, the greater effect It will have in shaping his or her worldview.

**The Challenge:**
Target one student and start a Bible study today. Write his or her name below.

_____

# R&R

**Read:** Exodus 20:1-21

**Focus Text:** Exodus 20:8 (KJV)
"Remember the Sabbath day, to keep it holy."

Typically, when we think of leisure or relaxation, we think of vegging out in front of your Macbook on YouTube, watching a bunch of movies, or playing hours of video games and eating a box of Count Chocula for lunch, all while sitting unbathed in footed pajamas the entire day. While there will be days you just need to sleep it off, by engaging in "active rest" you will recover in a more productive way.

What is active rest? Active rest is a rest method used by modern athletes to recover after strenuous training or competition. The old-school method of recovery used to be do nothing. (Think previous paragraph, footed Star Wars onesie and all.) However, research has shown that low to moderate-impact activity is more effective for maintaining strength and flushing out waste from muscles than just sitting around doing nothing.

Keeping your mind and body active during rest is the key to increasing recovery from high stress activity.

Here are a few active rest tips:

Keep up spiritual disciplines. The Holy Spirit is your source of strength and power. Spend time reading, reflecting, and praying on your rest days.

Engage in contrasting activity. Contrasting activity is doing something that is completely different from your normal routine. Going to a coffee shop to read, having your devotion in a park, reading some well-written fiction, or going out with some friends are all examples of activities that are typically in contrast to the daily routine of most student ministers.

Move around. Get outside or go to the gym, and move around. Whether you run an Ironman or just go for a walk around the block, moving around does wonders for your mind. Exercise causes your body to release endorphins and adrenaline in your mind. It'll relieve stress and make you feel good. So go make a move!

Be social or get alone. If you've spent your day surrounded by people, then spending some time away may be a good thing. This depends a lot upon your personality. If you recharge around people, then get around people, but not those you lead. Hang out with friends and ministry peers, and have some fun with them. If you're the kind of leader who is more introverted and finds social situations draining, getting away from everybody may be a good idea. Getting out into nature, reading a book, or taking part in some physical activity are some great ways to get away from the crowds.

The key to success in your active rest is moderation. Don't be afraid to move at a slower pace. The goal is to engage your mind and body with activities that are in contrast to your typical day.

**The Challenge:**
Rest and relax today. Come up with a couple of "active rest" ideas that will engage your mind and body. Most of all, enjoy your day off!

# MUSIC

**Read:** Philippians 4:4-9

**Focus Text:** Philippians 4:8 (ESV)
"Finally, brothers, whatever is true, whatever is honorable, whatever is just, whatever is pure, whatever is lovely, whatever is commendable, if there is any excellence, if there is anything worthy of praise, think about these things."

We all understand the power of music, but there are times when we fail to recognize its impact in our own lives.

Hold up! Don't close the book. We're not telling you that if you have anything other than Michael W. Smith on your iPod, you're somehow a puppet of the devil. We are saying that music has the power to transport your heart and emotions to all kinds of places. Some of those places are good, others are morally neutral, and some are nasty.

Philippians 4:8 commands us to keep our minds in the right place. In all forms of pastoral ministry, especially in the world of student ministry, there is a high amount of stress. It is total elation and victory, and total fight and struggle at the same time. Sometimes you just need to feed your mind some praiseworthy things that lift your spirits by lifting up Jesus. When you block out time for yourself to focus totally on things of honor and purity, it has a way of recalibrating your mind to get inspired!

Inspiration is not uncritically absorbing a resource. Rather, it's using what is around you as inspiration for the unique work of art that God will lead you to create.

In order to freshen things up we need to be inspired. As bivocational, or even full-time youth workers, we can get stuck in a rut, doing the same old thing week in and week out. The key is variety. The more resources you have at your fingertips the more diverse and prepared you will be.

**The Challenge:**
Visit a music store or go to iTunes, and buy a new Christ-centered album and just listen. Soak in a new God-experience. Write your thoughts about the music below.

_____

_____

# GENEROUS

**Read:** II Samuel 24

**Focus Text:** II Samuel 24:24 (ESV)
"But the king said to Araunah, 'No, but I will buy it from you for a price. I will not offer burnt offerings to the Lord my God that cost me nothing.'"

You've got lots of stuff. It's probably because you're pretty rich. "On my salary?!" you exclaim. Yep. You're pretty stinkin' loaded. Of course, if you're comparing yourself to celebrities on TMZ or Forbes richest list, or if you're looking at your neighbor's or your best friend's stuff, then, yeah, you can probably find a lot about your life to be dissatisfied with. We won't hit you with a torrent of stats about how rich you really are, but if you have a car to drive and enough food to eat, you are "wealthy" compared to the majority of the world's population.

We live in a culture that celebrates living even though it is in a constant state of want. How many times have you instantly felt discontent when a commercial debuted a new smartphone or a coveted "fruit-based tablet device?" We've all felt left out, unhip, and not cool anymore. It sounds so unbelievably shallow, but our culture is driven by the feeling that we don't have enough. We say we just like nice things, but Jesus calls it lust.

There is a reason you must break yourself of the selfish desire to have things. Until you do, there will be parts of your life that are only about you; you will do things primarily for what you get out of them. Yeah, you bought a homeless guy lunch, but you tweeted about it an hour

43

later. Sure, you spent some time with down-and-out kids in your ministry, but you were sure to remind them how busy you were and how special they should feel that they got to be with you. Maybe you didn't say that directly, but it was implied.

In our Focus Text, David was in trouble. He had made a bad decision. He had ordered a census to number his army, but his motivation for the census was his pride. He desired to raise his "street cred" so that everyone would know how awesome his army was. This ticked God off. God was handing out punishment options for this bad decision, and David chose the one that would impact his people over himself. Plague descended upon Israel, and 70,000 people died. In a vision, David saw more destruction coming, and he repented. Upon repentance, David's key to escaping trouble was to make a costly sacrifice. His unwillingness to pay for his sins had placed his nation squarely on the tracks of the oncoming train of the Lord's anger. The only way to stop the destruction was for David to sacrifice. What had gotten them in trouble in the first place was David's want, but giving a costly sacrifice was what turned back the curse.

Right now, ask yourself these questions: "What things do I covet?" "What do I desire that has the potential to bring me trouble?" Go ahead, be honest with yourself! Proverbs says, "Some people are always greedy for more, but the godly love to give!" (Proverbs 21:26 NLT)

We know this has been pretty direct, but the fact of the matter is, we've all felt the cold hand of greed and selfishness trying to grab hold of our ministries. We've all wanted more; more power, more influence, more recognition, and more love from those we lead. These things can taint our motives, but generosity stops our wants in their tracks.

**The Challenge:**
Give sacrificially in the next few days. It may be money, time, or a gift that you decide to give, but whatever it is, make it cost you something. Give without expecting gain. And no publicizing it!

Challenge suggestion:
Find a widow or a single parent in your church or community. Look at your bank account, and see how you can give sacrificially. Give, and let God do the rest.

# CONNECT

**Read:** Proverbs 27:17

**Focus Text:** Proverbs 27:17 (NLT)
"As iron sharpens iron, so a friend sharpens a friend."

Human connection and interaction are some of the most basic human needs. If you're a youth worker who never takes the time to contact or connect with other youth workers, you probably feel alone, a little burned out, and a bit stale creatively. At first, it may seem like a paradox to be surrounded by people and to still be alone, but ministry experts often state that pastoring is one of the loneliest professions on earth. Based on personal experience, many pastors believe that statement is true. Pastoring is a unique vocation. You never truly clock out. You carry the hopes, dreams, failures, and shameful secrets of countless people. You are expected to always be on your A-game, being the empathetic counselor, engaging communicator, fearless leader, active listener, and perfect example. There are very few people who understand the constant juggling of ministry and family along with the careful management of dozens of separate expectations. All of this is topped by a deep burden to see young people encounter Jesus and be discipled. In this environment you need friends who "get" you!

Brandon: "There have been many times throughout the years as a youth pastor that I was going through things not even my wife, my family, or my best friends could understand. But it was other youth workers I was connected with that I was able to reach out to in those moments of need. If you have never experienced one of these youth-pastor moments, just wait; you will. And when you do, you will need a network of intentionally developed friendships and peers."

If you want a network of friends, you've got to reach out. Go to conferences; connect with other youth pastors and leaders. Perhaps you've heard the old adage: "Your network is your net-worth." How true. Networking doesn't happen by accident; it takes hard work and hustle. Remember that relationships are give-and-take. If you're willing to put yourself out there and support others, then you will be supported too.

One of the keys to keeping your network fresh is connecting with people in the good times as well as the bad. We have a tendency to reach out only when things are not going well or when we need advice. If these are the only times you connect with your network, your peer-to-peer community will be pretty weak. Reach out frequently. Call or text just to see how someone is doing. The more you connect, the easier it will be to deal with "stuff."

**The Challenge:**
Take a minute today and connect with two or three other youth workers. Find out what's going on in their worlds and in their youth ministries. Ask them very specific questions. Make connecting a habit by contacting them once a week.

Below, list their names:

_____

_____

_____

_____

_____

# TRIANGLE

(Authors' note: The next three challenges are about facilitating relationships. This chapter contains no challenge but sets up the next three.)

Structural engineers tell us that the triangle is the strongest geometric shape; triangles have the ability to bear huge, heavy loads without becoming deformed. A triangle will not change shape unless its sides are bent or its joints are broken. In essence, each of the three sides supports the other two. Now before you breakout the Popsicle sticks and Elmer's Glue, we're not talking about constructing your next student center; but about your students. Think of yourself as a master engineer undertaking a massive construction project. Except the "thing" you're building is actually not a thing at all; it's young people. Like a bridge builder, you need to construct those you lead with strong support systems to help them withstand the pressure of being a follower of Jesus in the 21st century.

Teens and young adults carry a tremendous load as they diligently attempt to follow Christ in their culture. It is not always their friend. From entertainment to education, our students are fed a theology contrary to the Bible. They are told that they are the arbiters of their own truth and morality. Everything is constructed by culture and society, thus there are few, if any, moral absolutes. Sexual preference and gender identity are determined by the individual, and no church, pastor, or sacred Scripture has the right to determine what is morally absolute concerning human sexuality. Joy is determined by the amount of stuff you have. If you're a girl your value is determined by the perfect-ness of your body and the display of it to men so you can gain their approval. If you're a guy, your value is determined by your sexual prowess and the number of girls you've slept with. Sin is presented as an offensive, outmoded concept used by those in power to control those who follow them. Then there are the questions of destiny: "Who am I?" "What am I supposed to be?"

Young people face pressure, and as a youth worker you are tasked with making sure they can withstand and thrive in the face of pressure. One of your building materials is the "triangle" of relationships. Your job is to facilitate healthy relationships. If one of those relationships is unhealthy, students face a higher risk of collapsing under the pressure. There are three key relationships you must help facilitate. They are the relationships your students have with their parents, pastor and Christ. We will split up these three relationships over next three challenges.

# TRIANGLE 1

**Parents**

**Read:** Deuteronomy 6:1-8

**Focus Text:** Deuteronomy 6:7 (NIV)
"Impress them on your children. Talk about them when you sit at home and when you walk along the road, when you lie down and when you get up."

One of the most significant relationships you need to facilitate and strengthen is the one between youth and their parents.

Never underestimate the power of family. For good or bad, the state of relationship between parents and students in these formative years has the power to make or break their faith. Family dysfunction is a major stumbling block to healthy spirituality. Your job is to help students build healthy relationships with their parents.

Part of facilitating a healthy parent-student relationship is admonishing those you lead to honor the authority of their parents. It is important that you do your very best to never let your frustration with parents bleed into your communication. Damaging a student's view of his or her family can have a devastating effect on their emotional and spiritual health.

Another part of facilitating a healthy parent-student relationship is making sure that you have a good relationship with parents. If you've ever tried to work with a student, and it seemed you weren't getting anywhere, the reason may have been that you weren't listening to the parents.

Some youth pastors talk as if the parents of the youth in their ministry are their enemies. Yes, there is the occasional parent who thinks you can't get anything right. But the majority of them are genuinely in your corner. Parents are not your enemies! By building healthy relationships with parents, you get a snapshot of the needs of those you lead. Specifically, you get insight into how a youth acts at home and at school. Behavior at home is an indicator of character and what areas may need some work.

Brandon: "Once a year in my youth ministry, I would put together a think tank of parents. This was one of the greatest things I ever did as a youth pastor. When I started listening to what parents had to say, I found out my job got a whole lot easier."

What if the parent-student relationship is broken? We live in a broken world and sometimes family relationships break down. Marriages crumble, children rebel, or sometimes abuse erodes the integrity of the home. Whatever the reason, as a leader you must help students walk through the breakdown of the relationship with their parents. Ultimately, through your guidance, perhaps some professional counseling, and the grace of God, they can come through the experience whole.

If the relationship between student and parent breaks down, one of two things must happen. The relationship must either be repaired or replaced.

Repair: Sometimes during the teen years, youth rebel as they attempt to assert their independence. Hormones, especially in young men, run high and emotions can bubble over. During conflict, hurtful words can be rashly spoken by both parents and youth. This can place tremendous strain on relationships in a family.

In today's society, sometimes marriages crumble, mistakes are made, and even spouses are unfaithful to one another. Divorce and sexual immorality can wreak havoc on a family. Regardless of the cause or who is at fault, we should seek repentance, forgiveness, and restoration.

Replace: Sin sometimes breaks things beyond repair. Abuse or extreme circumstances may cause reconciliation to be impossible. While forgiveness should always be sought, certain acts done in a home are so heinous that the relationship forever changes. In those situations it is important that young people find parental care and mentorship in another godly, safe environment. This is where your solid relationship with the rest of your church family will pay off. You will be able to find caring, older adults who will become father and mother figures. While nothing can replace mom and dad, elders can provide guidance and examples that will serve to support a student's life.

**The Challenge:**
Contact a couple of parents in your youth ministry. Meet with them and trade vision. Find out what God-given goals they have for their students. Then reassure them that you are there to support that vision. Below, list a couple of parents you can connect with today.

_____

_____

_____

_____

_____

_____

# TRIANGLE 2

**Pastor**

**Read:** Titus 2:1-11

**Focus Text:** Titus 2:11 (NLT)
"For the grace of God has been revealed, bringing salvation to all people."

In *Silos, Politics, and Turf Wars*, Patrick Lencioni defines silos as: "The invisible barriers that separate work teams, departments and divisions, causing people who are supposed to be on the same team to work against one another . . . silos—and the turf wars they enable—devastate organizations by wasting resources, killing productivity, and jeopardizing results."[5]

Within any organization, the larger it gets, the greater the temptation for its various departments to isolate themselves from the larger body. It's easy as they become more self-sufficient and don't really need anyone else. This can happen easily within the Church as the various departments are completely geared towards specific needs or demographics. As team members in a department rally around each other to meet the goal of their department, they can become so focused on their mission that they lose sight of the fact that their vision is in context with the rest of the church.

---

[5]    Patrick Lencioni. *Silos, Politics, and Turf Wars.* http://www.tablegroup.com/books/silos/.

Whenever an organization builds silos, its clients suffer the most. They suffer because they lose vital connection to the whole of the organization.

In the Focus Text of this chapter, you read Paul's admonition to Titus to instruct each demographic of the church to act in a way that was complementary to the other. From the eldest man to the youngest girl, Paul states that we are to act in a way that honors the other so that maximum community can be built. Paul was combating the "silo effect" that can strike any organization. It's human nature to segregate and focus only on what's like you. The church is to be the antithesis of culture and go against the grain of human nature when it collides with Scripture.

You are a leader in God's Church, and you must be diligent that your youth ministry never becomes a silo. It is imperative that the rest of the Church, its departments, and its leadership are seen. Furthermore, your students need to feel a vital connection to their senior pastor.

The senior pastor is the one who sets the vision, builds the culture, and generally decides what kind of church yours is going to be. Seeing that the pastor is such an important figure in the leadership of the entire organization, your youth should feel a strong connection to him or her. By increasing the visibility of the senior pastor and the rest of the church, you help young people see themselves as part of a larger body filled with diversity.

**The Challenge:**
Book a date for your senior pastor to speak at a youth service.

# TRIANGLE 3

**Jesus Christ**

**Read:** John 3

**Focus Text:** John 3:29-30 (ESV)
" . . . Therefore this joy of mine is now complete. He must increase, but I must decrease."

Adam: "It was early Sunday morning. Like 5 a.m. early, which, at least when you're five, is obscenely early. I awoke to the sound of a single, familiar voice. I lumbered out of bed, and sleepily stumbled downstairs into the family room. There I found my dad kneeling next to the sofa in his tattered blue housecoat, passionately crying out to God in prayer. Beads of sweat popped on his forehead, and tears ran down his cheeks as he stood in the gap for every single person who would attend service that morning. This was not an uncommon sight in my home. My dad was, and still is, a spiritual giant. Growing up in a church planter's home we had to make some sacrifices. Sometimes we weren't able to go as many places or have as much stuff as others. Most of our expendable income was poured back into the Kingdom of God. But we were rich in the Holy Spirit. Both my mom and my dad did the greatest thing any leader could do for anyone who follows them; they pointed me to Jesus. My mom taught me the value of faithfulness, and my dad taught me the power of surrendering to the Holy Spirit."

In our Focus Text, John the Baptist is reaching the end of his ministry when his followers come and dejectedly announce that Jesus is attracting a larger crowd and baptizing his followers. Instead of responding in anger and jealousy that the humble Carpenter was now jacking his swagger, John responds with joy. He exclaims, "My joy is now complete, he must increase and I must decrease!" John is disappearing and the Christ is now being revealed. Since Jesus has come, John will now fade into obscurity and soon suffer the death of a martyr. Before we brush over this story as just another among thousands in scripture, let's not forget that John was a real guy who actually lived. And I know this may seem like a stretch, but imagine you are John. Go ahead, take a few seconds, close your eyes and let your mind wander back to the Judean wilderness. Imagine the surge of adrenaline you'd get while proclaiming to a culture who had turned their back on God that the Messiah is coming! Crowds numbering into the thousands travel long miles to hear you preach. They line the muddy banks of the Jordan River to have you, yes, you baptize them. What a rush! Now picture all of that going away. All of your followers leaving you for a new guy. Your freedom is slipping away and you are about to suffer the humiliation of being beheaded at the request of a stripper. And all of this is the will of God. Would you be ok with that?

The fact is, we are not building our own kingdoms. We are to be paving the way for our King and declaring his Kingdom has come. The last portion of our triangle that will anchor young people and help them withstand pressure is their relationship with Jesus Christ. Like John, we are to simply be a voice crying out in the wilderness, paving a pathway for students to encounter the Messiah. As facilitators of healthy spiritual relationships, developing ways for youth to encounter God—both inside and outside the church—is key. Youth need to be taught to pray, fast, study scripture, and witness, and they need to be encouraged to do these things. It's up to you to best make that happen in your local context.

**The Challenge:**
Create a survey of spiritual disciplines for your students. Ask basic yes/no questions, with one or two short-answer questions, about their prayer and Bible reading habits, and whether or not they feel they have enough resources to help them with their spiritual growth. Study the

results. Where are the gaps, and how can they be addressed? If most students are struggling with prayer and Bible reading, devise a plan based on the feedback you've received that will assist them in their spiritual growth.

# GRATEFUL

**Read:** Ephesians 4

**Focus Text:** Ephesians 4:19-20 (NLT)
"So now you Gentiles are no longer strangers and foreigners. You are citizens along with all of God's holy people. You are members of God's family. Together, we are his house, built on the foundation of the apostles and the prophets. And the cornerstone is Christ Jesus himself."

Everything comes from something.

Adam: "Whether you're talking about a good cup of coffee, a car, a life on planet earth, or the success of your ministry, nothing just pops into being. Everything comes from something. This includes your ministry. Are you a great communicator? God gave you that gift. As talented as you are, someone paved the way for you to get where you are now.

"This is why it bugs me when I see my generation of ministers knocking the elder generation. It reminds me of adolescents knocking their parents' wedding photos. Yeah, a blue velvet tuxedo on your dad is kind of weird. Sure, your mom's perm makes her look like a French poodle. However, without "Blue Velvet Suit" and "Awkward Hair" getting together, there would be no you. Likewise, without those so-called old, seemingly out-of-touch, uber-traditional elders, there would be no church for you to lead. Cut them some slack and be grateful for their sacrifice!"

Brandon: "In the summer of 2005, my beautiful wife and I were installed as the youth pastors at Christian Life Center in Stockton, California. As a pastor with a lifetime calling to youth work, this appointment was definitely one of the highlights of my ministry. Leading up to the appointment, I had served as assistant youth pastor for two years under the leadership of Eli Lopez.

"During my tenure in Stockton, I pastored more than 300 students each year. The youth ministry was called 'Acts-twenty9,' and we were a rockin' group. As hundreds of teens passed through our doors each year, I made sure each student was discipled. This was not a youth ministry driven by events; rather it was driven by relationships. Choosing health over hype was a priority and it showed.

"Today, so many of the students who graduated from Acts-twenty9 are spiritually healthy and still living for God. Many of the youth have gone on to fill different offices in the five-fold ministry. Some have become worship leaders, pastors, musicians, and mighty soul winners.

"With what most consider success, it would be easy to pat myself on the back and say, 'Brandon, job well done. You sure knocked it out of the park with that one.' But the truth is, I stood on the shoulders of giants—the men who went before me who paved the way for my effectiveness. They were men like Kenneth Haney, Jeff Garner, Simeon Costa, Eli Lopez, and many others. They poured themselves into that local youth ministry long before I was youth pastor. They invested tirelessly and fearlessly, and it was because of them that I had the success I did.

"I will never forget them. I am grateful for those men. The day I despise or mock those who have gone before me is the day I undermine my future as a leader. Every single one of us, at some point in life, has benefited from those who have gone before us. From those who built organizations and churches, to those who personally invested in us, they laid a foundation that we are honored to build upon. For those men and women we are grateful."

**The Challenge:**
List a few people you are grateful for and contact them in the next few days. Let them know how much you appreciate them.

_____

_____

_____

_____

# DELEGATE

**Read:** John 4:1-26

**Focus Text:** John 4:6-8 (NLT)
"Jacob's well was there; and Jesus, tired from the long walk, sat wearily beside the well about noontime. Soon a Samaritan woman came to draw water, and Jesus said to her, 'Please give me a drink.' He was alone at the time because his disciples had gone into the village to buy some food."

Whether you're a seasoned youth worker or a rookie, delegation is one of those tasks that never ends, and if you're not careful, it can be difficult to pull off. However, if you can master this critical skill in personal effectiveness, the dividends are enormous.

Brandon: "As mentioned in another challenge, you cannot do it all! My wife Amy owns and operates a small business with around eight employees. Her business does very well, and she is amazing at what she does. She is such a major go-getter. This quality is one of the many reasons I fell in love with her and ultimately married her. (Husband-points!) Even though her business is small, one of her challenges has been delegation. Often, she bites off more than she can chew.

A while back, a framed sign in the 'keep-calm-and-carry-on' tradition showed up at our home. The sign read: 'I cannot do it all.' I loved it! This was her declaration that even though she wanted to do it all by herself, and probably could have, she was going to delegate. This simple act made her a much more effective leader. And, trust me, our home has been a happier place because of it."

You cannot do it all!

There are a few mindsets you have to get rid of if you're going to properly delegate.

Shed the mindset that says, "If you want it done right, then you have to do it yourself." Truthfully, that statement is really all about your ego. Another truth is, you're not the only person who can do this job right, and chances are, you're not the only person who can do this job right now. Put your ego aside. Have the patience and take the time to train somebody to do the job properly.

Another mindset you have to lose is waiting for people to jump in and help. Most people, in general, are not like you: you see a need, and you jump in without being asked. This is why you are in leadership. Of those you lead, most are interested in helping, but they are waiting for an invitation. So go ahead and invite them! Ask, and you shall receive.

Avoid the urge to micromanage. Once you've delegated a task to someone, let it go! Give him or her the opportunity to become a capable leader. Think back to a time when you were just starting out, and somebody gave you the opportunity to grow by allowing you to succeed, or perhaps fail, at a delegated task. Yes, the person you delegate to will make mistakes. It is a part of the learning process. Your job is to be patient and not get frustrated.

At the end of the day, don't forget to recognize people for the work they have done. Whether or not it was done exactly as you would have done it, always, always say, "Thank you."

Here's how you get started.

First, identify the things that only you can do. Our Focus Text records the famous story of the woman at the well. You've probably heard a variety of messages preached from it. For the purposes of this chapter, Jesus' role in the story was possible because he had delegated the task of getting food for the day to his disciples. If Jesus had been busy doing a Chik-fil-a run for "the twelve," then his life-changing encounter with the woman at the well would never have happened. This is why, no matter how lean your staff is, you need to find ways to delegate. Do only what only you can do! For example, being a husband or a father is something only you can do. Crafting biblically sound messages that help young people live for Jesus is something only you can do. Preaching is a priority.

Next, identify the things that anyone (or almost anyone) can do, such as organizing a day at the park or running the soundboard (this one takes a lot of patience), then delegate those tasks to capable volunteers.

As you delegate, you will have time to focus on building up your strengths. When you're constantly doing menial tasks on your own, then your focus is on your weaknesses. You are not able to use your strengths as a leader doing the things that only you can do.

Before we go further, ask yourself these questions: "What are my strengths and weaknesses?" "Where am I, and where am I not, talented and gifted?"

**The Challenge:**
List three things you are going to delegate this week.

_____

_____

_____

# TRUST

**Read:** Colossians 3:5-11

**Focus Text:** Colossians 3:9 (NLT)
"Don't lie to each other, for you have stripped off your old sinful nature and all its wicked deeds."

Here's a question, do people trust you? Do you do what you say you will do? Yes, you're well organized. You can preach like a machine. You know how to smile and shake the right people's hands, but are you trustworthy? You will not be successful if those you lead do not trust you. If they do not trust you, they will not believe in you, they will not confide in you, and they will not depend upon you.

Trust is essential in youth ministry. Our young people come to us at times with very little trust in people. Marriages crumble, life isn't fair, and sometimes people are betrayed. Thus, the truthfulness of our words and deeds are our currency. The hard part about it all is that losing trust is easy. It's gaining it back that can be tricky and difficult. This is why you must learn to practice the discipline of confidentiality. As a leader, people will come to you with the pain and dysfunction of their lives. As they prepare to pour out their hearts to you, assure them that what they're about to say will stay with you. Confidentiality will not only protect your integrity, it may also protect your church legally from liability.

The only time confidentiality should be breached is when you discover someone is in danger or about to make a life-altering decision that will affect the spiritual, emotional, or physical health or safety of themselves or others.

Adam: "In the developing stages of the student ministry at my local church, we enacted a confidentiality statement and instituted reporting procedures in cases where the information must be passed on to proper authorities. I'm glad we had these things when problems hit. When you're in the middle of a crisis, having prepared systems ensures that nothing you are legally and ethically obligated to do gets missed."

If you earn people's trust, you also earn an excellent reputation. You will find that you spend less time trying to persuade people to follow you. Your ministry will run more smoothly, and people will have less reason to attack and criticize you.

Here are five trust rules:

1. Make solid promises. Never promise something you're not positive you can deliver.

2. Keep your promises even in the small things. By starting small, people are more likely to believe you can keep your word on the big things.

3. Keep your word even when it's difficult. There will always be an excuse for why you couldn't come through. Instead, you have to find an excuse for why you can deliver.

4. Hold others accountable for the promises they make to you. As you do this, you will begin to attract other honest and dependable leaders who will help you focus on the more important issues.

5. If the promise you are making is too difficult to remember, create a paper trail. With today's technology, there are so many ways to document an agreement, whether via voicemail, text, email, etc.

**The Challenge:**
Make the commitment that from today on you will live your life with honesty and integrity. If there is someone, or even multiple people, whose trust you may have lost, go to them today and begin to "mend the fences."

List those people below.

_____

_____

_____

_____

# VALUE

**Read:** Luke 19:1-10

**Focus Text:** Luke 19:5-6 (NIV)
"When Jesus reached the spot, he looked up and said to him, 'Zacchaeus, come down immediately. I must stay at your house today.' So he came down at once and welcomed him gladly."

Think back to a time when someone stopped and told you how valuable you are. Maybe it was a conversation in passing, or maybe they took the time to take you out for coffee. By the end of the conversation, you felt like you were on top of the world. Why was that?

From the text we see that Zacchaeus was a wealthy man as well as a tax collector. And as we all know, even in modern times, the IRS is not very popular. I'm sure being wealthy as well as a tax collector didn't make Zacchaeus very well-liked either. I can imagine how despised Zacchaeus felt as a person. But, one day Jesus passed by and noticed Zacchaeus. Jesus made Zacchaeus feel important and valued by inviting himself over for dinner. That was a major compliment in those day. We see immediate results in Zacchaeus by looking at his response: "But Zacchaeus stood up and said to the Lord, 'Look, Lord! Here and now I give half of my possessions to the poor, and if I have cheated anybody out of anything, I will pay back four times the amount.'" (Luke 19:8)

Right then and there Zacchaeus was ready to change not only his lifestyle but his system of values. He was sold hook line and sinker because Jesus took the time to recognize his worth. How many people are around you just waiting to be valued?

Look around you; are there Zacchaeus-type people on your staff? You have volunteers who will eagerly follow you to the ends of the earth if you will simply take the time to recognize them and their value.

One of the habits of great leaders is that they understand how to make people feel valuable, not just once or twice, but continually. The best way to build and attract a hardworking loyal staff is to value people.

You value people by being present when you are with them. Being present means that during the time someone spends with you, they feel like they have your absolute, undivided attention.

Here are some tips for being present:

Fight the need to respond. You don't need to react to every comment; only speak when you can add genuine value to the conversation.

Make eye contact. Looking someone in the eye is a sign that you are engaged with what the person is saying. We're not suggesting you adopt a creepy stare, but as they speak, looking them solidly in the eye lets them know you are paying attention.

Isolate yourself from distractions. Ignore your phone, ignore your phone, ignore your phone. Get the picture? Seriously; ignore your phone.

**The Challenge:**
Reflect on the last time someone made you feel valuable. What did they do? What did they say?

_____

_____

_____

As a leader, you need to create that same feeling in the lives of your staff. Connect one-on-one with three members of your youth staff. Somewhere in the conversation, express to them that you value them.

Whom will you contact?

_____

_____

_____

# VISIT

**Read:** Acts 2

**Focus Text:** Acts 2:42-44 (NKJV)
"And they continued steadfastly in the apostles' doctrine and fellowship, in the breaking of bread, and in prayers. Then fear came upon every soul, and many wonders and signs were done through the apostles. Now all who believed were together, and had all things in common."

In his book, Outliers, Malcolm Gladwell relates the amazing story of the Rosetans, a group of Italian immigrants living in Roseto, Pennsylvania, in the 1950's. It was reported to Dr. Stewart Wolf, by a local doctor, that heart disease did not exist in Roseto and that its citizens lived longer than normal lifespans. Dr. Wolf researched the phenomenon and determined that neither diet, exercise, genetics, nor location was the key to their longevity. He noted how the citizens interacted and cared for one another and did not isolate themselves. For example, multiple generations lived in the same house, people often stopped on the street to chat, and neighbors frequently ate meals together. Civic centers abounded and each person, regardless of social position, was made to feel equal to everyone else. Dr. Wolf concluded that the Rosetans' secret was their sense of community.

Sin separates us from God and keeps us from good relationships with each other. But Jesus Christ died and rose again, making restitution for our sin. When we are born again, we are reconciled to God and to each other via the Church.

The outpouring of the Holy Spirit on the Day of Pentecost was not just a great spiritual revival, it was the advent of a new way of life. Through the Holy Spirit, the members of this new church began to actively care for and reach out to one another, especially to those with needs. Leaders and people of influence began building authentic community, bringing people together.

This means that your presence in the lives of your youth outside of church is also valuable. You are more than just a public speaker. Your students don't just value your ability to expound on a text, they value you. Thus, when you show up at a ball game, a school play, or a graduation, you do the work of an Acts 2 leader and build community and connection. The same is true when you invite others into your life. Transparency in ministry is so important. As leaders we often teach and preach on what we should do but not on how to do it. Living for God is no mystery; its success is found in your daily routine.

The challenge: (Pick one or as many as you would like.)
Visit a local high school today. Of course, you'll need permission from the school office. Go at lunchtime, or as the students are leaving for the day.

Find out who in your youth group is on a sports team or performing in a play. Go watch them and cheer them on. You'll make their week.

Invite a youth to join you on an errand today. It doesn't have to be anything special or spiritual; just get with them, and let them see the real you.

# PULL THE TRIGGER

**Read:** Acts 15

**Focus Text:** Acts 15:36-39 (NLT)
"After some time Paul said to Barnabas, 'Let's go back and visit each city where we previously preached the word of the Lord, to see how the new believers are doing.' Barnabas agreed and wanted to take along John Mark. But Paul disagreed strongly, since John Mark had deserted them in Pamphylia and had not continued with them in their work. Their disagreement was so sharp that they separated. Barnabas took John Mark with him and sailed for Cyprus."

Brandon: "I hold a contractor's license in the state of California. My wife and I ran a small fencing company for several years before I was full-time in ministry. Hiring too hastily and firing too slowly were two lessons I learned the hard way."

Learning the art of "pulling the trigger" is an essential leadership skill. Being the senior leader of a department or ministry will require you to make the difficult executive decisions. Hiring and firing are among the most stressful situations a leader can undertake. The key to success is thinking through a situation before you make a decision. However, the need to take an appropriate amount of time for consideration should never be an excuse for making no decision.

When you delay firing the wrong person, you delay the opportunity for God to work something new and different in that person's life. Conversely, when you delay hiring the right person, you take away a chance for your organization to thrive and grow. Every time you hire too quickly you set your organization up for setback and you set yourself up for future awkward conversations.

## The Hire

Before you ask someone to be part of the team, you need to ask yourself two questions. Is there a need to be filled, and, is this the right person for this job? Just because you like someone doesn't mean you should hire him or her. You will frustrate yourself and them if there is nothing for them to actually do.

Once you've found a need to be filled, the next task is ensuring you've found the right person for the job. The right person will have the proper skills and good character.

By "proper skills" we mean that they have the technical competency or potential to do the job with excellence. For example, if you're looking for a new person to join the choir, you need to ensure that they can sing. And nothing says "awkward service" like a tone-deaf worship leader or a drummer who can't stay on beat. We're not implying that unless someone is a genius they can't be part of the team. Sometimes people are not where they should be technically even though they demonstrate real potential. Part of good leadership is realizing someone's potential and assisting them in becoming the best they can be.

The kingdom of God is too important to have to deal with tons of drama. This is why you must choose people of good character. If they have a history of not controlling their emotions, maybe they're not ready for leadership yet. The same could be said if they not ethical, are prone to gossip, or are sexually immoral. God will never lead you to choose people who willfully violate his word and are hypocrites. While we all make mistakes and have flaws, as a leader you must make a distinction between a person honestly trying his or her best and a carnal person who is unsubmitted to Christ.

Once you find a need to be filled and the right person to fill it, then pull the trigger and hire them already!

The Fire

Sometimes things just don't work out. People misuse their authority, fall into sin, or stop caring, or sometimes they just aren't the right fit. Sometimes you just have to pull the trigger and fire them.

Adam: "I used to manage a retail store before I was hired full-time by my church. As a manager, I was responsible for staffing the store. This meant at times I had to let people go. While it wasn't an enjoyable experience, it wasn't that hard. I just told them if they were no longer needed or had violated certain policies, and then I took their keys. That was it. It wasn't personal; it was business. When I got on staff at my church, I had to let someone go from one of our volunteer teams. This was a good person, who, it turned out, was just not ready for leadership. That firing was a completely different experience. I was anxious, my stomach was in knots, my palms were sweaty; I was scared! I was terrified because church isn't like a business. It's always personal. People put their hearts on the line because the church is a network of deeply personal and communal relationships. Since firing someone from a church position is radically different from the business world, it must be approached with compassion and reverence.

Here are some keys to letting someone go the right way:

Never fire in anger. Sometimes things can get intense. When they do, it is important that you keep a lid on your emotions. Never make any major decisions when you are angry.

Fire someone only as a last resort. Before you remove someone from a ministry team or leadership position, exhaust all other opportunities to retrain or redirect the individual. Termination is final. Give him or her multiple opportunities to change.

Embrace that this will be painful and awkward. If all attempts to rehabilitate a non-functioning team member fail, then perhaps it's time to let that person go. When you do, understand that it will be a painful and awkward conversation for you both. Don't try to run away from it; embrace it as one of the necessary evils of working with people.

Use the communication sandwich. Invite the individual into your office or some other private place. After exchanging some small talk, begin by complimenting and thanking them for their service to the team. Then announce your decision to remove them from the position. Outline why you're making this decision. Be honest. Tell what they've done wrong, what corrective steps you've undertaken, and how these steps have not worked out. If you've attempted to work with them before now, then this decision should not come as much of a shock to them. End by affirming both God's love and yours for them. This conversation should be short. Don't drag it out.

Help them find a new area of service or ministry. If there is any place that should preserve the dignity and worth of a person, it is the Church. The key to firing yet preserving someone's self-worth is restoration. Restore by helping them find a new place of meaningful and vibrant service. Or, if they have been let go for moral reasons, oversee their restoration to spiritual wholeness. Never fire someone and then walk away. Continue to be a force for good in his or her life.

**The Challenge:**
Ask God if anyone on your leadership team needs to move on. Also ask him to replace that person with someone who needs to be there.

# LEGACY

**Read:** John 19:23-27

**Focus Text:** John 19:26 (NLT)
"When Jesus saw his mother standing there beside the disciple he loved, he said to her, 'Dear woman, here is your son.' And he said to this disciple, 'Here is your mother.' And from then on this disciple took her into his home."

Jesus is at the end of his life. He's on the cross, and about to take his last breath. Standing at the foot of the cross are some of his devastated followers. Among them are his mother and his closest disciple, John. Despite the agony of the cross, Jesus looks down and hands his mother off to John. The care of one's mother was an important duty for a son. The mother was a valued member of the family; her gift of providing life made her special. Now that Jesus is about to die, he passes this great responsibility to John.

This story brings up some important questions. Are you preparing for the future? Do you have an apprentice to replace you? Do you have someone to take your special young people and lead them when you're gone? I've known many youth pastors who did not have their replacement determined, so they ended up serving longer than they ever intended to. When they left they were burnt out, and their youth ministry was burnt out too.

You can do some crazy damage by not considering your legacy. The future of the youth ministry is important, so it is foolish to think only about how things currently are while you are around. In the grand scheme of things you are just a feather in the wind.

When you understand that your position is only temporary, you will be okay with saying, "Hey, this person whom God has chosen to be leader after me might not be a carbon copy of me, but that's okay. I might do some things better than he does, and he does some things better than I. I'm okay with that because this isn't about me, it's about the Kingdom."

When you ignore legacy and the next generation, you are actually hurting your ministry. You are potentially doing future damage to the young men and young women you love and serve. Legacy is not about how you will be remembered. It's bigger than that. It's about the youth ministry continuing to thrive after you are gone. It's all about the sustainability of your youth ministry.

Just look at how Jesus set up the next generation in his own ministry. he put in place a structure, and he gave Peter the "keys to the kingdom."

**The Challenge:**
Write down how you want to be remembered as a youth minister. What will your legacy be? Write down a clear definition of what success in youth ministry means to you.

# DREAMS

**Read:** Genesis 42:1-9

**Focus Text:** Genesis 42:9 (NLT)
"And he remembered the dreams he'd had about them many years before . . ."

Brandon: "I still remember the day when my mother asked me what I wanted to be when I grew up. The year was 1985, and I was five years old. Michael Jackson had just come out with the song 'We Are the World,' and Nike had just released the first pair of Jordan's. For me, the world was a place full of wonder and dreams.

"Let's take a trip down memory lane. What were some of your childhood dreams?

Here were some of mine. I wanted to:

- Be an astronaut, which meant being in zero gravity
- Fight in a war as a U.S. Marine
- Be the President of the United States

All very easy and doable, right?"

For the sake of this challenge, let's define the word "dream" as "a goal or aspiration that God has placed in your heart that you deeply long for or desire."

Brandon: "As I travel and survey youth today, here are some of the dreams I see:

- Build wells in Africa
- Make lots of money to be independently wealthy
- Obtain a doctorate
- Go on a cruise
- Write a book
- Pastor
- Have a successful career
- Own a business
- World peace
- Play in the NBA"

The truth is, we all have dreams. But life, job, school, family, friends, church, ministry, and dream-killers can bury our dreams.

Here is a list of dream-killers. Can you identify with any of these?

- Lack of road map
- Disinterest
- Obstacles and problems
- Circumstances
- Procrastination

If your dreams can be buried, then they can be dug up. God has given you the tools to do this.

What would this challenge, on the subject of "dreams," be without mentioning Joseph, the greatest dreamer of all time? Here are a couple of things we learn from Joseph's life.

First, he defined his dreams. Know what you truly desire and be very specific in the details of the dreams you want to fulfill. Articulate them. Write them down! Prioritize them.

When you prioritize and organize, it promotes definition. Use whatever tools you have to help you fulfill your desired dreams. On your computer, or in a journal, place all the specifics of your dreams. This might include pictures, diagrams, or contacts' names and phone numbers. As you consider your dream, add to this list.

Get prepared. Be ready to walk into your dream. There is a well known saying: "Luck is when preparation meets opportunity." It's true; opportunity will come to everyone who is prepared. Will you be prepared?

Second, Joseph shared his dreams, and you've got to share yours. Think about it. Joseph's dreams would never have been fulfilled if he had not shared them. It was the very act of sharing his dreams that set things in motion and prepared the way for the fulfillment of the dreams God had given him.

Remember, you cannot get there alone. You need to have people helping you along the way. Don't be afraid to ask others for help and criticism. When people give you feedback, cherish it and use it. Anyone can be criticized or corrected; rare is the person who can listen to correction and benefit from it.

Sharing your dreams always makes you accountable to them. The more you share, the more you will feel the positive pressure to focus on fulfilling your dreams.

Third, Joseph stayed in the process. We never see him dream again, but he didn't abandon the process. Dreams can change. They can become bigger or even smaller. My childhood dreams were just seeds for bigger things. Dreams are not elusive or unattainable, but rather, the product of everyday life. The secret to achieving your dreams is found in your daily routine. Sometimes the prison is part of the process. Stay in the grind!

Fourth, Joseph helped others. Even though he never dreamed again, he helped others with their dreams. On the road to the fulfillment of your dreams, stop and take the time to help others. The help that Joseph provided to those around him, made the fulfillment of his dreams possible in ways he could never have predicted.

In summary, Joseph was a dreamer. His brothers didn't understand his dreams. They didn't like his dreams; they hated them so much that they staged his death and sold him into slavery. Joseph survived because he clung to his dreams. He remained effective and embraced the grind, because he knew that every day he was getting one step closer to the fulfillment of his dreams. You must get a dream/vision from God. Dream of big things in your life and ministry. Those dreams will fuel you in difficult and trying times. Dreams will cause you to love the grind and embrace radical productivity. Keep your dreams out in front.

**The Challenge:**
Write down the dreams God has given you for your youth ministry. What would you attempt if you knew you could not fail? If you had no financial limits, what dream would you accomplish? Be specific! Draw a sketch of what it looks like.

# REPEAT

Famed Filipino, Manny Pacquiao, didn't become the world's most fantastic lounge singer and boxing champion overnight. It was through hours and hours of drill, practice, and hard work. You've reached the end of the book, but not the end of the journey. The challenges you have successfully accomplished are designed to become habits that will grow your leadership and deepen your character.

Embrace the grind.

**The Challenge:**
Repeat the 29 challenges

# References

1   Denis Howe. noise.Dictionary.com; *The Free On-line Dictionary of Computing*. http://dictionary.reference.com/browse/noise.

2   Denis Howe. nausea.Dictionary.com; *The Free On-line Dictionary of Computing*. http://dictionary.reference.com/browse/nausea.

3   "Noise pollution" *Wikipedia, the free encyclopedia*. http://en.wikipedia.org/wiki/Noise_pollution#cite_note-0.

4   Mike Esterl. "A Frosty Reception For Coca-Cola's White Christmas Cans". http://online.wsj.com/article/SB10001424052970204012004577070521211375302.html. (accessed May 30, 2012)

5   Patrick Lencioni. *Silos, Politics, and Turf Wars*. http://www.tablegroup.com/books/silos/.

CPSIA information can be obtained at www.ICGtesting.com
Printed in the USA
LVOW12s0757170315

430799LV00001BA/40/P